SURPLUS

SURPLUS

TITANIC

TITANIC

Revised & Updated Edition

Frank Sloan

RSVP

RAINTREE
STECK-VAUGHN
PUBLISHERS
A Steck-Vaughn Company

Published by Raintree Steck-Vaughn Publishers, an imprint of Steck-Vaughn Company

Cover Design: Gino Coverty
Project Management, Design & Electronic Production: Gino Coverty
Media Researcher: Claudette Landry

Library of Congress Cataloging in Publication Data
Sloan, Frank
    Titanic / Frank Sloan
        p.   cm.
    Originally published: New York : F. Watts, 1987.
    Includes bibliographical references and index.
    Summary: Describes the ocean liner Titanic, its maiden voyage and sinking, and discusses the recent discovery and exploration of the ship's remains on the ocean floor using deep-diving robots and the representation of the Titanic on stage and in film.
        ISBN 0-8172-4091-8
        1. Titanic (Steamship) — Juvenile literature.
    [1. Titanic (Steamship)   2. Shipwrecks.]   I. Title.
    G530.T6S58   1998
    363.12'3'091631 — dc21   98-14034
                                                                                        CIP

Printed and bound in the United States
1 2 3 4 5 6 7 8 9 0 LB 02 01 00 99 98

Photograph Acknowledgments
Cover: © Antonio Jacobsen/Christie's Images; p. 2 © Montague B. Black/Christie's Images; pp. 6-7 © Antonio Jacobsen/Christie's Images; p. 10 AP Photo/Michael Caulfield; pp. 16-17 Movie Stills Archives; p. 21 Brown Brothers; pp. 26-27, 32-33 Brown Brothers; p. 35 Popperfoto; p. 42 Culver Pictures Inc.; p. 48 UPI/Corbis-Bettmann; p. 52 Brown Brothers; p. 55 Corbis-Bettmann; p. 58 Corbis-Bettmann; pp. 65, 70 Movie Stills Archives; p. 75 © Ralph White/Corbis; pp. 82-83, 84 © Woods Hole Oceanographic Institution; pp. 88, 91 (both) © Ralph White/Corbis; p. 92 Reuters/Greg Box/Archive Photos; p. 99 AP Photo/Adam Nadel p. 102 © Ralph White/Corbis; p. 110 © Leonard de Selva/Corbis.

CONTENTS

...And as the smart ship grew,

In stature, grace and hue,

In shadowy silent distance

grew the iceberg too.

Alien they seemed to be

No mortal eye could see

The intimate welding of their

later history.

From *The Convergence of the Twain*,
by Thomas Hardy

TITANIC

PROLOGUE

March 23, 1998

Today, in Los Angeles, California, the Academy of Motion Picture Arts and Sciences gave the Academy Awards for the best movies released in 1997. It was the seventieth anniversary show. One of the biggest movies ever made—in every sense of the word—walked away with eleven Oscars, including the highly coveted award for Best Picture: James Cameron's *Titanic*. In February of 1998 the movie had been given fourteen Oscar nominations, tying the record of 1950's *All About Eve*, for the largest number of Oscar nominations ever given. *Titanic*'s eleven-Oscar sweep made its win a tie with 1959's *Ben-Hur*, for the greatest number of Oscars given to a film in one year.

Cameron himself was given an award as Best Director. Among the other awards given to *Titanic* included Best Cinematography; Best Film Editing; Best Art Direction; Best Costume Design; Best Original Dramatic Score; Best Original Song; Best Visual Effects; Best Sound; and Best Sound Effects Editing.

Academy Award nominee Kate Winslet joins James Cameron for a moment of congratulations during the Oscars ceremony on March 23, 1998.

The evening, Hollywood's annual party to celebrate its place in the world, was even longer than Cameron's film, but at the end, when Cameron accepted his award for best picture, he moved the glittery audience by asking for a moment's silence to honor the 1,500 people who died when the ship went down. Despite being a motion picture filled with multimillion-dollar pyrotechnics, *Titanic*, as James Cameron proved to the audience packed into the Shrine Auditorium, is a drama about people.

All in all, it was a night to remember...

The story of the great ship's sinking has been an immensely popular one since that fateful voyage when the *Titanic* sank shortly after striking an iceberg in the North Atlantic while on her maiden voyage to New York. The ship was the largest moving object in the world.

For eighty-five years, the world had longed to know exactly what had happened to the *Titanic*. During all that time, adventurers had wondered precisely where the ship was and what kind of shape it was in. Would the wreck, once found, yield up untold treasures? Were there still bodies on the ocean bottom, preserved in the dark waters? What would the years of silence disclose?

This is the story of that ill-fated voyage and what has been learned about it since 1912.

A MILLION TO ONE

Shortly before midnight on Sunday, April 14, 1912, the largest liner in the world struck an iceberg in the North Atlantic. A little more than two and a half hours later, Great Britain's R.M.S. *Titanic* sank, and around 1,500 people lost their lives. The *Titanic*'s sinking was the worst maritime disaster ever to take place during peacetime, and it was one of the most incredible accidents that could have occurred. Many people had described the liner as unsinkable. No one believed that anything could cause the *Titanic* to sink. And no one could foresee that it would happen on the grand ship's maiden voyage, or first Atlantic crossing. The odds against the *Titanic* going down were probably a million to one.

The event took place more than eighty-five years ago. The world was different then. The twentieth century was just twelve years old. The British Empire was at its height, and America had emerged from the nineteenth century as a power to equal any in the world. Radio and television didn't exist. Women had not yet won the right to vote. The automobile was still a rare and luxurious item. World Wars I and II hadn't been fought. There was an air of innocence and confidence all over the world. And people, including many immigrants who had just arrived in America, were full of hope for the future. But at the same time there was also widespread political unrest, poverty, and unhappiness.

The impact of the *Titanic*'s last hours was enormous. The deaths of so many people were of great interest to the general public. Many of the passengers on the ship were wealthy and some were famous. They were like the rock and movie stars and sports celebrities of today. And in 1912 the liner they traveled on represented the last word in technology and progress.

Steamships had been crossing the Atlantic on a regular basis since the 1840s, and many well-known and popular liners carried people back and forth. The rich traveled on fast ships, tasteful floating hotels that re-created the most luxurious and glamorous hotels and public buildings on land. In the days when ocean travel was popular, ships almost took on personalities, much the way people today like to stay at the same hotel—sometimes in the same room—over and over again.

Wealthy passengers traveled on the upper decks of ships. They had luxurious staterooms and elegantly decorated public rooms where they could amuse themselves during the voyage, which could last from seven to fourteen days.

But the poor traveled in third class in the bottom and the back of the boat, where the noise and motion were most noticeable. This part of the ship was called steerage, and the quarters were often filthy and cramped. It was known as steerage because cattle had once been carried there on the trip from America to Europe. And immigrants were herded in like cattle on the return voyage. Most of these people were on their way to the land of opportunity, to build new lives in America, and getting there made any conditions they had to endure worth it.

WHERE DOES THE STORY BEGIN?

Where and when does the story of the *Titanic* really begin?

Does it begin in the late nineteenth century? In those days there were neither jets nor propeller-driven airplanes that could cross the Atlantic in a matter of hours. There was a need for large ships to carry travelers between America and Europe. And ships were the only way to go. Bigger and bigger ships were needed all the time to transport the people from Europe who wanted to emigrate and settle in America.

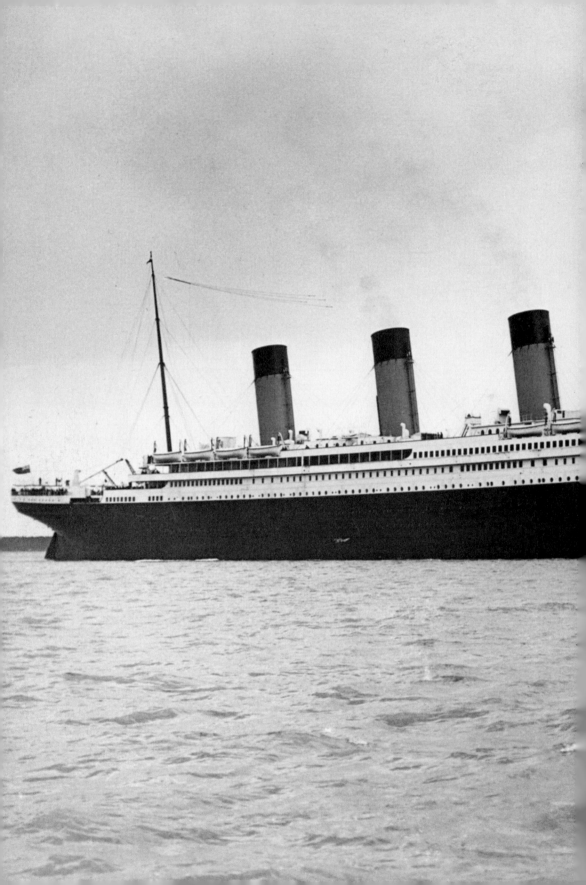

Or does the story begin in 1902? That is the year when the American financier J.P. Morgan and other investors formed a group called the International Mercantile Marine. This company would eventually purchase the White Star Line, the *Titanic*'s owners, for $25 million in gold.

Or does it begin in 1907, the year that saw over 1,200,000 immigrants arrive in the United States? There was competition among the steamship lines to carry the most people. They all knew there was a great deal of money to be made from the immigrant traffic. And the steamship lines needed ships to carry these immigrants.

In that same year, the Cunard Line introduced its two large luxury liners, the *Mauretania* and the *Lusitania*. In just a short while these ships became the most popular boats crossing the Atlantic. They were popular because they were the fastest ships afloat. The White Star Line, Cunard's great rival for transatlantic passengers, had no ships as big or as fast. The company wanted to outstrip Cunard's popular ships with luxury liners of its own. So the owners of the White Star Line began to dream. And the company's designers and naval architects began to plan for the future.

Perhaps the story begins when two momentous things happened on the same day. On May 31, 1911, the *Olympic*, the White Star Line's brand-new flagship, began her maiden voyage from England to America. At almost the same time of day, the *Olympic*'s slightly larger sister ship, the *Titanic*, was launched at the Harland & Wolff shipyards in Belfast, Northern Ireland. Even the name, *Titanic*, suggests greatness: it comes from the word titan, which stands for a race of giants. Neither White Star Line ship would be faster than the *Mauretania* and the *Lusitania*, but each one was larger. And they would be the most luxurious ships afloat.

When the *Titanic* was launched on that spring day in 1911, the ship was far from complete. During the next ten months, the great ship was fitted out. This means that the masts and funnels were added. The interior electrical equipment and boilers that ran the ship were also installed. And the final touches were put on the sumptuous interior decorations.

Or does the story of the *Titanic* begin as the great liner left Great Britain on its maiden voyage? The ship steamed majestically away from the dock in Southampton, bound for Cherbourg, France. There she would pick up additional passengers and then head for Queenstown, Ireland. At Queenstown the ship would make a last stop and pick up further passengers for the seven-day voyage to New York.

The date was Wednesday, April 10, 1912.

2 THE GREAT SHIP SAILS

The maiden voyage of the *Titanic* began uneventfully enough at noon on that April 10. Because of a coal strike in Great Britain, there was confusion about when the new liner was going to sail. The *Titanic* needed an unheard-of 650 tons of coal a day to keep her boilers at full steam. To save coal to use on board the *Titanic*, other ships had canceled their sailings. The *Titanic*'s passenger list was not full. In fact, she was filled to only about 60 percent of her passenger capacity.

As the ship left her Southampton dock, everything seemed to be working beautifully. But then something unexpected—and almost unfortunate—happened. As the *Titanic* passed two other vessels moored side by side at their pier, the suction from the *Titanic* pulled one of the vessels loose. The *New York* pulled away from the *Oceanic* and narrowly missed crashing into the side of the departing *Titanic* by just a few feet.

The **Titanic** *narrowly escaped collision as she left Southampton. The suction of her propellers tore the American liner* **New York** *from her moorings.*

Captain E.J. Smith of the *Titanic* used his head and quickly ordered a round turn and stopped the *Titanic*'s engines. As her propellers stopped, so did the suction. This got the *Titanic* out of the other ship's path, and the new liner was on her way. Disaster had been narrowly averted.

To many on board, including the crew, the near miss seemed an ominous beginning. And in years to come this small incident would take on significance as an example of the *Titanic*'s "bad luck." Even before that accident, twenty-two men who had signed on as crew members disappeared and never showed up. There were whispers that she was an unlucky ship.

Some people even said the *Titanic* was jinxed because she had a mummy in the hold, a mummy that carried a curse with it. Others spoke in hushed tones of a great Buddha with an evil spell. Hidden in Captain Smith's safe, it too was supposed to symbolize bad luck.

VITAL STATISTICS

A ship's maiden voyage always caused great excitement. And because the *Titanic* was the world's largest ship, this was a particularly momentous occasion. She was known as R.M.S. *Titanic*, for Royal Mail Ship. Indeed, on her first and only trip, the *Titanic* carried almost 3,500 bags of mail in addition to 900 tons of baggage.

The *Titanic* measured 46,328 gross tons, which made

her 50 percent larger than any other boat afloat. Gross tonnage is the most common manner of "weighing" a ship. It is actually a cubic measurement of size. And "she" and "her" are the traditional nautical pronouns used to refer to a ship.

The *Titanic* was 883 feet (260 m) long from front to back. This is about the same as four city blocks. The ship was 92.5 feet (30 m) wide in the middle, the widest part. From her keel, or bottom, to the top of the bridge (the highest part of the superstructure) she measured 104 feet (30 m), almost as high as an eleven-story building. She cost over $10 million in 1912 money to build.

The *Titanic* had four majestic smokestacks, or funnels. In the heyday of great ships a four-stacked liner was a symbol of elegance and luxury. Three of the funnels were actually used for carrying off smoke and steam, but the fourth was a dummy and was used as a ventilator. Each smokestack averaged 62 feet (19 m) high and was 22 feet (6.5 m) across. Two train locomotives, side by side, could fit in each funnel.

Because she had a double bottom the great liner was heralded as "unsinkable." This meant that the hull was constructed with two coats of steel, one inside the other. She also had sixteen watertight compartments. Even if, by some extraordinary circumstance, as many as two of these compartments were to fill with water, the ship could still remain afloat.

The *Titanic's* sister ship, the *Olympic*, had been in service for almost a year and in that short time had become popular with North Atlantic travelers. But the *Titanic* had a few features the *Olympic* didn't have. The front end of the promenade deck on the *Titanic* sported glass windows. This was almost a necessity for sheltering passengers on the often frigid crossing. The *Titanic* also had a set of staterooms on B deck with real windows, not portholes. The *Titanic* offered a café on B deck that was designed to give passengers the feeling of dining at one of the sidewalk cafés of Paris.

The ship was divided into three classes: first, second, and third. Most of the space on the ship, especially in the middle of the ship and on the upper decks, was given over to first class. Second class held the smallest number of passengers and had simple but tasteful public rooms on upper decks, toward the rear of the ship. Third class (steerage) passengers were given modest space furthest down in the boat. Although steerage on the *Titanic* was plain, it was clean, which it emphatically wasn't on some of the Atlantic ships. Single men in third class were segregated from the women—each at opposite ends of the ship. Families were allowed to sleep together. On this crossing, as on most voyages to the United States, many of the immigrants had come from all parts of Europe and spoke little or no English.

Third-class passengers had very little deck space and their public rooms were small but comfortable. Gates were set up between the accommodations to keep the classes from mingling. It was strictly forbidden to go from second or third classes into the first, although it was a traditional shipboard "game" to try and do so.

GETTING USED TO THE SHIP

The passengers spent most of the first day settling in and making themselves comfortable for the voyage. They were getting used to the ship and getting to know as many of its luxurious features as possible. After all, this was a ship whose fittings equaled those of the most elegant buildings on shore. The spacious public rooms were parlors furnished with deep carpets, pianos, easy chairs, and great sofas.

Shortly after the ship got under way, stewards were busy setting up deck chairs in the outdoor spaces. Not long after that pots of steaming tea and small sandwiches and cakes would be passed around. Active people could work out in the gymnasium or indulge in games of shuffleboard on spacious outdoor decks reserved for first-class passengers.

Most of the passengers in first class were wealthy Americans, including heirs to some of the country's

greatest fortunes. The *Titanic* and the *Olympic* had been
built with Americans in mind, while the *Lusitania* and the
Mauretania were extremely popular with British travelers.
The passenger list contained people with a total wealth
of more than a quarter of a billion dollars. Many of the
wealthiest first-class passengers had maids or valets to
unpack the great numbers of trunks and suitcases that
would be needed during the trip.

Looking toward the rear of the Titanic. The open deck space at the extreme stern of the ship was meant only for third class passengers.

Not only were the passengers getting used to the ship, but so were the crew members. Because the *Titanic* was a new and important ship, the crew had been picked very carefully. The White Star Line had spared no expense in staffing the *Titanic*. Of the 900 crew members, about 500 were stewards and maids who worked above decks, constantly on duty, seeing to the passengers' needs. They were like the staff of a grand luxury hotel. And after passengers went to sleep at night, cleaners readied the ship for the next day. Chefs, waiters, and busboys all staffed the various kitchens and dining rooms. There were nine "bootblacks" whose only job was to be sure that all the passengers' shoes were polished. Two small orchestras, one made up of five musicians and another of three, played soft popular melodies in the background.

Far down, at the bottom of the ship, were the "greasers," the engineers and stokers. These were the men who shoveled coal into the ship's great furnaces to keep her steaming at such a fast speed. And everywhere else, throughout the ship, were the officers. These men, ranking just under the captain, were responsible for supervising the rest of the crew. They all worked together to make sure the ship was running smoothly.

Two of the crew members whose names would become well known a short time later were busy in the wireless room. Also known as the Marconi station, this small room at the top of the ship was staffed by John G. Phillips and Harold Bride. Their biggest job was to receive radiograms, also known as radiotelegrams or marconigrams, which told passengers what was happening on land. They also, of course, sent telegrams back to land. Radio telegraphic transmission was, in 1912, a fairly new science. No one dreamed that in a few days it would save many lives.

On the top decks, in sumptuous luxury, there were some very distinguished passengers: Isidor Straus, the department store owner, and his wife, Ida; the Philadelphia financier George Widener; President Taft's military aide, Major Archibald Butt; and the financier Benjamin Guggenheim. One of the world's richest men, Colonel John Jacob Astor was on board with his new wife, Madeleine. They were anxious to get to New York, so Mrs. Astor could give birth to their first child in America.

One first-class passenger whose name would become even more well known in time to come was Mrs. Margaret (or Maggie or Molly) Brown, the outspoken wife of a Denver millionaire. Kind but brash, Molly Brown was not completely accepted on board by her fellow first-class passengers.

Other important first-class passengers included Jacques Futrelle, a writer and contributor to the Saturday Evening Post; theater manager Henry B. Harris; the popular artist Francis David Millet; William T. Stead, a spiritualist and an editor; and the engineer Washington Augustus Roebling, who had been responsible for building the Brooklyn Bridge.

One of the other prominent passengers was Bruce Ismay, the managing director of the White Star Line and one of the few men to survive the sinking of the *Titanic*.

As the most distinguished representative of the White Star Line on board, he had good reason to be proud of the new ship. Although the *Titanic* wasn't due in New York until the following Wednesday morning, there was some feeling that Ismay would urge Captain Smith to speed the vessel in order to arrive late Tuesday evening and thereby generate even more publicity for the ship's first Atlantic crossing.

LUXURY AT SEA

First-class passengers paid $4,350, or about $50,000 in today's money, to stay in one of the *Titanic*'s elegant suites. The cost of passage included meals in the dining rooms. Only drinks and specially ordered food were extra. The one-way fare for second-class passengers was $65 and up. Steerage passengers paid an average of only $35 for the chance to cross the Atlantic.

The first-class public rooms were spacious and elegantly fitted out with mirrors, crystal light fixtures, and potted plants. There was a great lounge and a smoking room, usually reserved for male travelers. An enormous dining room (or dining saloon, as it was called in those days) was on D deck. It was as wide as the ship itself and could seat over 500 people at one time. In addition, the ship featured a restaurant, where very special and private meals could be served—at considerable additional cost.

The kitchens on board were among the best equipped and most modern to be found anywhere.

The *Titanic*'s four elevators had richly carved wooden paneling; the palm court featured an elaborate trellis with plants twined around it; and there was even a Turkish bath. Pets were kept in a kennel where they could be visited by their concerned owners. A separate lounge was provided for the maids and valets of the wealthy passengers.

By evening on the first day, the *Titanic* had crossed the English Channel to France. The ship was too big to dock in Cherbourg. A smaller boat, called a tender, brought the new passengers to a spot just outside the harbor entrance where the *Titanic* was anchored. Within a few hours the passengers and their baggage had been loaded and the ship was under way once again.

The next morning, on Thursday the eleventh of April, the ship was approaching Queenstown, Ireland. There she would make a last stop before heading out into the Atlantic and crossing to New York. By 1:30 P.M. the *Titanic* had loaded her final passengers and was under way.

To the best of anyone's knowledge there were 1,316 passengers and 892 crew members on board, for a total of 2,208 people. Because the exact records went down with the ship, a completely accurate count will never be

(on following page) The grand staircase on the Titanic.
The staircase in James Cameron's movie is a close replica of this.

known. There may have been some passengers without tickets and some people who made last-minute changes. There may even have been a stowaway or two. Most sources report a total between 2,201 and 2,224 people on the *Titanic*.

By the morning of the twelfth the *Titanic* was well out in the Atlantic and sailing along at a speed of 21 knots. Knots are used to measure the speed of boats. One knot is one nautical mile per hour. A nautical mile is the same as 6,076 feet (1,852 m). It is slightly more than a mile on land. Although 21 knots does not sound like a very fast speed to us today, in 1912 it made the *Titanic* a very speedy ship. And even today the fastest ships do not travel much faster.

The weather was fine, and the food and company were excellent. Passengers pronounced the ship a great success. The seas were calm and there were almost no cases of seasickness. And the ship herself performed well. There were very few complaints about vibration caused by the ship's engines or about rolling, two things that often made oceangoing passengers uncomfortable.

Everyone had settled in, and the ship was becoming more like a luxurious home to most of the first-class passengers. A pattern was established of easy days

Captain Smith looks down from the starboard bridge while the ship is anchored at Queenstown, Ireland. One of the sixteen wooden lifeboats can be seen suspended from its davits.

followed by gourmet meals and evenings of dancing and card playing in the lavishly decorated public rooms. This routine was expected to continue until the ship arrived in New York, where she was due on Wednesday, April 17.

Passengers enjoyed the indoor swimming pool and the squash racket courts. Both of these were novelties on a ship and were very popular. A newspaper was published every morning on the *Titanic*. Specially prepared and printed on board the ship, it was called the *Atlantic Daily Bulletin*.

The ship was described by some—and with good reason—as a magnificent moving hotel, a floating city.

THE SHIP HITS THE ICEBERG

3

On Sunday evening the fourteenth, life was slightly quieter than usual. Religious services had been held earlier in the day. There had been a hymn sing in the dining room following dinner and, because it was a Sunday, dancing was not permitted. Card-playing would not normally have been allowed on an English ship on a Sunday, but perhaps because it was the ship's maiden voyage, some of the stricter rules had been relaxed.

The ship's speed had been increased slightly to 22.5 knots. The sea was calm, and during the course of the day, people had noticed that the weather was getting colder. By nightfall the temperature had dropped considerably, but the skies were clear and moonless.

Many of the passengers had gone to bed. Only a

few die-hards were still up, having a last cigarette in the smoking room or playing a final hand of cards.

At 11:40 P.M. a few people on the upper decks noticed a slight jar. As described by one writer: "...the ship seemed to shake herself—just like a wet dog."

Most of the passengers didn't even realize that anything serious had happened, let alone that the *Titanic* had just struck a floating mountain of ice. It had all happened in a matter of ten seconds. A few people rushed out on deck and saw pieces of ice on the ship's decks. Some claimed they had seen an 80-foot-high (25 m) iceberg receding into the distance off the back of the starboard (right) side of the ship. For a long time, there was no concern: after all, the *Titanic* was unsinkable! Most first-class passengers slept on, and few realized that the next several hours were going to change their lives in all kinds of ways.

Who had spotted the iceberg? Two men were in a small bucketlike affair called the crow's nest that was fastened about halfway up the front mast. These men were called lookouts, and their responsibility was to let the captain know as soon as possible if they saw any problems. They did see the iceberg, but not until it was too close to avoid the collision.

Most of the passengers were not aware that several times during the course of that Sunday, April 14, there had been warnings that the *Titanic* might come across ice in some form or other. There had been messages all day long from several other ships in the area. These messages stated that there was dangerous ice nearby. Although Captain Smith and his officers knew of the potential danger, most of the messages were ignored.

Many of the passengers also didn't realize that when the boat struck the iceberg, some part of the ship below the waterline had been wrenched open. Water was rapidly filling the lower parts of the *Titanic*. For most of the last eighty-five years people had assumed that a 300-foot-long (90 m) gash had been ripped, as if by a can opener, along the lower part of the hull. Whatever the cause, the wound to the vessel was severe.

The nightmare had begun.

THE BEGINNING OF THE END

A deathwatch had begun. Captain Smith knew it, and so did many of his senior officers. As soon as the collision occurred, the captain ordered the ship to be stopped. This took nearly four minutes, and the ship traveled almost half a mile (0.8 km) before she was fully stopped. Although alarms were immediately sounded and the doors between the watertight compartments were shut, within ten minutes water had flooded the first three holds to depths of about 14 feet (4 m).

The watertight compartments at the bottom of the ship's hull had begun to fill with water. Why? Simply because the compartment walls, or bulkheads, weren't high enough. The ship began—slowly at first—to sink from the bow, or front. As one compartment began to overflow, the one next to it would then begin to fill up. And this pattern was repeated from the bow back to the stern, or tail, of the ship.

Captain Smith understood the severity of the accident. Smith was a distinguished veteran of thirty-eight years at sea. This was to have been his last voyage before he retired. Smith knew the ship was in trouble because he was an experienced sailor. He also knew because Thomas Andrews, the naval architect who had overseen the *Titanic*'s design, had told him. Andrews was on board and had been one of the first people to rush down to the bottom of the ship after the accident. There he had found water pouring in at a rate that was too fast for the pumps to carry it away. His training and instinct told him the ship could not survive.

The crew below deck were the next people to grasp the extent of the damage. They worked desperately to keep the water out. They managed to keep the electricity on board the ship running almost until the very end. This made the work of abandoning the ship safer and more orderly than it might otherwise have been. Since there was no need to keep the ship's engines running, every person turned to the task of pumping out the increasing flood of water. The engineers stayed below deck as long as possible.

Some other people who knew the severity of the accident were Harold Bride and John Phillips, the two wireless operators. Up in the wireless room they had been given instructions to begin sending distress calls.

By fifteen minutes after midnight on the fifteenth, the *Titanic* had sent out a distress call: "Have struck an iceberg. We are badly damaged. Lat. 41.46 N., long. 50.14 W." A second call, shortly after the first one, repeated the message, but also included the new SOS (save our ship) signal. There is some uncertainty about whether or not the *Titanic* was the first ship to use the signal. Some sources indicate that the *Arapahoe*, in trouble in 1909, had been the first. In any event, the *Titanic*, if not the very first ship, was one of the first ships to use the SOS signal.

LEAVING THE SHIP

Most of the passengers still weren't aware that the ship was sinking. Many people had begun to assemble on deck in their life preservers. But they still felt there was no danger. After all, although it was very cold indeed, the sea was calm and there were even stars in the sky! But Captain Smith knew the worst. He knew the ship was doomed, and by 12:30, less than an hour after the

collision, he had ordered all passengers to gather on the boat deck. Women and children would be helped into the lifeboats.

Captain Smith was also aware of another fact: there weren't enough lifeboats for all the passengers. The ship had roughly 2,200 persons on board. A quick count of the fourteen 30-foot-long (9 m) lifeboats, two 25-foot-long (7.5 m) ones, and the four collapsible "Englehardt" lifeboats showed that their combined capacity, if fully loaded, was only 1,178. This meant that even if all the boats were loaded to capacity, almost a thousand people could not be accommodated. They would have little chance of survival in the icy sea.

Even at this point, there was little panic. People began to sense that the great ship was in trouble, but they remained calm. Crew members were assigned to help people into lifeboats. But because the ship was new, many of the crew were not used to the *Titanic* and weren't sure what to do. Due to the crew's uncertainty, many of the boats took a long time to lower.

Some of the boats were lowered half full, largely because many passengers weren't prepared to take the situation very seriously. As well, the crew was afraid that if the lifeboats were full, the added weight would cause these boats to crumple while they were suspended over

A painting that shows one of the lifeboats being lowered. The boat is filled with members of the crew and women passengers.

43

the side. The crew was on a new ship and didn't realize that the lifeboats were among the few things that had been checked out carefully.

On a ship like the *Titanic*, the lifeboats were stored, covered by tarpaulins, on the top, or boat, deck. They were attached to upright metal poles, called davits, with a system of ropes and pulleys. Crew members would unfasten the boats and move them out over the sea. The boats would be lowered down one deck. Then passengers could, with great care, step into the boats. Finally the boats would be lowered further, all the way down to the sea. But the operation requires practice to be performed smoothly.

And that is what had been missing. There had not been any lifeboat drill on the earlier days of the voyage. A common practice on all ships, lifeboat drill was something Captain Smith appears to have been lax about. As a result, people didn't know which boats they had been assigned to or how to get to these boats quickly in an emergency.

As they stood shivering on the deck that was beginning to tilt, the bewildered passengers began to realize that they might have to be inconvenienced and leave the ship. The calm was almost unearthly. Touching good-byes were said. Some of the men knew they were saying last farewells to their families. Some did not, and genuinely believed they would be reunited in just a few hours. Some women refused to be parted from their husbands and preferred to remain behind to face whatever might happen. Legend tells us that Mrs. Isidor Straus would not leave her husband, saying they had been together too long to be separated now. They then joined hands and sat side by side in deck chairs.

As the lifeboats were lowered, passengers began to get into them. Order prevailed as boat after boat, containing women and children and only partially filled, left the ship. Because the crew was inexperienced and poorly organized, the lifeboats could not all be lowered at the same time. Stories have come down of pistols being used to keep men out of the boats, of a man who dressed up as a woman in order to gain entrance to a boat, and of bribes being offered by wealthy people. But most accounts emphasize that there was little panic or confusion.

One of the wooden lifeboats to leave the *Titanic*, boat number 1, was lowered with only twelve people. It had been designed to hold forty. The four collapsible boats were awkwardly stored, very far away from the edge of the ship. They had to be shoved, with great difficulty, and placed into empty davits.

THE LAST HOURS

One by one distant ships responded to the distress signals. The Cunard Line's *Carpathia*, closest by, changed her course. Headed for the Mediterranean, she quickly answered the *Titanic*'s call and began to speed 58 miles (78 km) toward the sinking ship. But she was older and slower and wasn't used to going faster than about 14 to 16 knots. It would be, Captain Arthur H. Rostron estimated, almost five hours before she could get to the liner. And there was still ice to worry about and watch for.

As the *Titanic* began to sink from the front, the remaining passengers made their way to the rear of the ship, where they felt they would be safest—and farthest away from the approaching water.

And what happened to the steerage passengers? There were reports that they had been forcibly held back in their quarters. Stories were told of gates being shut, keeping these third-class passengers in dimly lit companionways. Some stories told of crew members keeping steerage passengers prisoner in their own quarters until most of the boats had been launched. And there are some disturbing statistics: while all the children in first and second class were saved, two-thirds of those in steerage went down with the ship. While almost all the women in first class survived the sinking, nearly half of those in third class did not.

By the time all the boats had been lowered, the ship had already begun to sink noticeably from the front. When the engineers from below finally left their posts and made their way to the top of the ship, all the lifeboats had been launched. For these brave men, it was too late. On the stern of the ship, passengers clung to whatever seemed permanent and fixed. Otherwise they would have been washed into the icy water.

The ship's orchestra had combined, and now eight musicians played ragtime melodies during much of the evacuation in an effort to cheer up worried passengers. Legend says they played the hymn "Nearer My God to Thee" as the ship went down, but there is some doubt about this. For one thing, this is an American hymn, and the melody would probably not have been familiar to English musicians. Also, every effort was made to keep people's spirits up, not to remind them that they might be about to die. Orchestra leader Wallace Hartley and his men played on the promenade deck until the players had to seek a drier spot, when they went up to the boat deck.

Lights continued to burn, the sea was calm, and from a distance it must have seemed as if nothing was wrong. But the line of lights blazing from the portholes and windows began to tilt more and more as the stern of the ship rose further and further out of the water. The great ship was definitely going down.

4

SINKING AND RESCUE

It was almost 2:20 A.M., Monday, April 15. As the angle of the ship became more and more vertical, her three propellers swung out of the water. The angle increased to 50, then 60 degrees. Even as the ship began its final plunge, few people jumped from the stern. Some witnesses insisted that the lights on board the ship stayed lit until just minutes before the vessel slid beneath the waves.

Just before that happened, a great roar went up. It was the sound of all the movable objects sliding noisily to the front of the tilting ship. Some witnesses remembered hearing the noise that one of the *Titanic*'s

A reasonably accurate painting showing the Titanic's last horrifying moments, as the stern lifted above the frigid North Atlantic waters. In fact, the lights most likely had gone out shortly before the ship plunged to the bottom of the ocean.

giant boilers made as it rolled from a position in the middle of the ship to the front.

Some people also recalled that the ship seemed to break in two, and that the forward part of the ship disappeared first and more quickly than the stern portion. Some eyewitnesses recalled that the funnel farthest forward toppled loose when the *Titanic* sank. Others seemed to remember that it came loose as that part of the ship met the water.

Between 12:45 and 1:45, eight white rockets had been lighted and sent up into the sky. These are the universal signals for ships at sea when they are in trouble. There is, to this day, dispute as to whether or not a British ship named the *Californian* was near enough to have seen the rockets and answered the distress calls. But the *Californian*'s captain had already gone to bed and the wireless had been shut down for the night.

There was a strong fear that the sinking vessel would create suction when it went down. This might pull the lifeboats under with it. As a result every effort was made to get the lifeboats as far away from the ship as possible. This may be one reason why few survivors were actually rescued from the sea. Only about a dozen people found floating in the water were picked up by any of the eighteen lifeboats that had been launched from the *Titanic*. With the sea temperature around 28°F (-2°C), few survived for very long. In fact, most of the bodies recovered showed that people had died from exposure, not from drowning.

THE RESCUE SHIP

Meanwhile the *Carpathia*, her engines pushed to full speed, was rushing to the scene. When she got there, at four in the morning, there was no sign of the *Titanic*. There was a floating field of wreckage and there were all the lifeboats. About 850 of the *Titanic*'s passengers had left the ship in lifeboats, and 705 of these were squeezed on board the *Carpathia*, which was, luckily, only half full. They came aboard the *Carpathia* by whatever means was practical or possible: ladder, boatswain's chair, slings, and bags.

For four hours the *Carpathia* combed the waters near where the *Titanic* had gone down. James Bissett, the *Carpathia*'s second mate, tells this story:

> *Our immediate task was only too clear—to search for the people in boats or rafts, and any other survivors. The increasing daylight revealed dozens of icebergs within our horizon. Among them were four or five big bergs, towering up to two hundred feet above water level. One of these was the one that the* Titanic *had struck.*

When the last lifeboat had come alongside the *Carpathia*, those who survived began to grasp the

A lifeboat full of
Titanic *survivors*
pulls alongside
the rescue ship,
the Carpathia.

magnitude of the tragedy. With a sense of horror the women and children on the rescue ship began to comprehend that their husbands and fathers had gone down with the *Titanic*.

Just before the *Carpathia* began her sad voyage back to New York, Captain Rostron positioned his ship over the spot that was assumed to be where the *Titanic* had gone down. When his ship was there, he and the rescued passengers paused for a service. This memorial was to commemorate those who had lost their lives during that fateful night.

THE WORLD WAITS

Radio communication was then very new, and there was a great deal of confusion in both the United States and England about the fate of the *Titanic*. Because of garbled messages, several newspapers reported that all the passengers had been saved and the ship was being towed to Halifax, Nova Scotia. Both the *New York Evening Sun* and the *Boston Evening Transcript* made this error. Only *The New York Times*'s information was accurate from the beginning. That paper correctly sensed the real situation and devoted its entire front page to as many of the details as were known.

In both London and New York, people who had heard rumors of the maritime disaster crowded outside the

White Star offices, demanding full explanations. Although it was known within about twenty-four hours that the ship had sunk, it took almost a week to compile an accurate list of all the survivors. When the final tally was made, the list was printed in newspapers and posted in hotels, public buildings, and large stores.

When the *Carpathia* finally arrived in New York City on Thursday night, April 18, it was in a driving rainstorm. More than 30,000 curious onlookers jammed the area near the pier. It took several hours to get the survivors off the ship and to clear the pier. Then the survivors began to give their firsthand recollections of the sinking. The same as it had been on the *Titanic*, the steerage passengers left the *Carpathia* last.

One person in the crowd, however, made his way *on* to the *Carpathia*. He was Guglielmo Marconi, the inventor of the wireless. Marconi wanted to congratulate the radio operator who had been able to send messages from the *Titanic* to the *Carpathia*. It was then that Marconi met Harold Bride, who had survived the sinking. Without a doubt Marconi's invention was responsible for saving as many lives as were saved.

The legend had begun.

TITANIC SINKS FOUR HOURS AFTER HITTING ICEBERG; 866 RESCUED BY CARPATHIA, PROBABLY 1250 PERISH; ISMAY SAFE, MRS. ASTOR MAYBE, NOTED NAMES MISSING

Col. Astor and Bride, Isidor Straus and Wife, and Maj. Butt Aboard.

"RULE OF SEA" FOLLOWED

Women and Children Put Over in Lifeboats and Are Supposed to be Safe on Carpathia.

PICKED UP AFTER 8 HOURS

Vincent Astor Calls at White Star Office for News of His Father and Leaves Weeping.

FRANKLIN HOPEFUL ALL DAY

Manager of the Line Insisted Titanic Was Unsinkable Even After She Had Gone Down.

HEAD OF THE LINE ABOARD

J. Bruce Ismay Making First Trip on Gigantic Ship That Was to Surpass All Others.

The Lost Titanic Being Towed Out of Belfast Harbor.

CAPT. E. J. SMITH,
Commander of the Titanic.

Biggest Liner Plunges to the Bottom at 2:20 A. M.

RESCUERS THERE TOO LATE

Except to Pick up the Few Hundreds Who Took to the Lifeboats.

WOMEN AND CHILDREN FIRST

Cunarder Carpathia Rushing to New York with the Survivors.

SEA SEARCH FOR OTHERS

The Californian Stands By on Chance of Picking Up Other Boats or Rafts.

OLYMPIC SENDS THE NEWS

Only Ship to Flash Wireless Messages to Shore After the Disaster.

PARTIAL LIST OF THE SAVED.

Includes Bruce Ismay, Mrs. Widener, Mrs. H. B. Harris, and an Incomplete name, suggesting Mrs. Astor's.

Special to The New York Times.

CAPE RACE, N. F., Tuesday, April 16.—Following is a partial list of survivors among the first-class passengers of the Titanic, received by the Marconi wireless station this morning from the Carpathia, via the steamship Olympic:

LATER REPORT SAVES 866.

BOSTON, April 15.—A wireless message picked up late to-night, relayed from the Olympic, says that the Carpathia is on her way to New York with 866 passengers from the steamer Titanic aboard. They are mostly women and children, the message said. It concluded: "Grave fears are felt for the safety of the balance of the passengers and crew."

Special to The New York Times

CAPE RACE, N. F., April 15.—The White Star liner Olympic reports by wireless this evening that the Cunarder Carpathia reached, at daybreak this morning, the position from which wireless calls for help were sent out last night by the Titanic after her collision with an iceberg.

THE PROBABLE LOSS.
Number Aboard.

First cabin	330
Second cabin	320
Steerage	750
Crew (estimated)	940
Total	2,340
Saved	
By the Carpathia	866
Probably drowned	1,354

5

THE
INQUIRIES

Just two days after the *Titanic* sank, the U.S. Senate authorized a full-scale investigation of the accident. Under Senator William Alden Smith, the examining committee was to look into the causes of the disaster. Some sense needed to be made out of what had happened during that three-hour period on April 14 and 15. An attempt was made to separate the legend from the truth, the myth from the reality.

In the American press, the British were made to look foolish. But the British got back at the Americans, when Senator Smith, in front of the Senate, made many grammatical errors and showed his lack of knowledge of the sea.

THE AMERICAN INQUIRY

It may seem strange that the U. S. government should be the first to set up an inquest. But many of the *Titanic's* passengers had been wealthy Americans. And the shipping line was, for all intents and purposes, owned by a group of American financiers. A lot of prominent Americans had gone down with the *Titanic*, and the public demanded explanations.

Over the course of several days, many passengers who survived were called on to testify. Among them was Bruce Ismay, director of the White Star Line and one of the few male passengers who survived the sinking. Several crew members also served as witnesses, including officers from the *Californian*. This was the ship that allegedly had neglected to answer the *Titanic's* calls for help.

No one attracted more attention than Second Officer Charles Lightoller, the highest-ranking officer on the *Titanic* to survive. Much of his testimony was extremely helpful. According to Lightoller, it was common practice to maintain speed on the North Atlantic, even with severe ice warnings. Much of what Lightoller said, and the way he presented himself, helped explain Captain Smith's interest in not slowing the vessel down. Lightoller's testimony also enhanced the White Star Line's credibility.

Under oath, Lightoller was asked at what time he had left the ship. "I didn't leave it," Lightoller replied. "Did it leave you?" asked a senator. "Yes, sir," Lightoller replied.

Several valuable points were brought out during the course of the lengthy trial. The British Board of Trade

was held responsible for the fact that there weren't enough lifeboats. The board's regulation stated only that a ship over 10,000 tons should carry sixteen lifeboats. The ruling made no provision for the fact that the *Titanic* was more than four times that size and would carry a great many more passengers (if not four times more) than a 10,000-ton vessel could manage. Due to this peculiar loophole, the White Star Line had acted within the law in equipping the ship. It was just that the law itself was senseless. The ship had been certified by the Board of Trade to carry as many as 3,547 people. But legally the *Titanic* only had to provide lifeboats for just 1,000 passengers.

There seems to be some evidence that the White Star Line deliberately chose to put too few lifeboats on the *Titanic*. The steamship company was afraid that if the boat deck was littered with too many lifeboats, first-class passengers would be deprived of their rightful open deck space.

Some people felt that the presence of Ismay on board had influenced Captain Smith's performance. Under this pressure Smith might have become overconfident, feeling he had to maintain the *Titanic*'s top speed. He was aware that there was ice in the region, and there should have been an order to slow the boat down. At the Senate

Bruce Ismay, on the right, on his way to testify at the British hearings. With him are his wife, Florence, and White Star Line general manager Harold Sanderson.

hearings, Ismay the survivor tried to shift as much responsibility as possible onto Captain Smith—the deceased. Ironically, when the fuss about the *Titanic* was over, so was Ismay's career. A broken man, he gave up all his business ties and became a virtual recluse. Interestingly enough, no officer who survived the sinking was ever given a command of his own.

The inquest also found that the ship had not been designed carefully enough. It soon became evident that the watertight compartments were anything but watertight. The quick and careless inspection of the vessel during her sea trials was cited as another shortcoming.

Because inspection had been inadequate and lifeboat drills had not been held, the loading and lowering of the lifeboats had been a haphazard affair. It was revealed that the men on lookout in the crow's nest did not even have binoculars. If they had had binoculars, would they have spotted the iceberg soon enough to have missed it?

Finally, the inquest raised the very serious question of the *Californian*. Where was this ship when the *Titanic* sent off its signal rockets? Had the *Californian*, as many people believed, been much closer to the troubled ship than the *Carpathia*? And wouldn't many more lives have been saved if the *Californian* had rushed to help the rapidly sinking liner instead of turning a deaf ear?

THE BRITISH VERSION

In fact, the position of the *Californian* during the *Titanic*'s last hours became a focal point of the British inquiry, which began on May 3, 1912, and continued for over a month. Almost a hundred witnesses testified during the course of the hearing.

The British investigation stressed the lessons to be learned from the tragedy. The purpose of the inquiry was to find out what had gone wrong so that it couldn't happen again. There was no interest in placing blame, especially on a captain who had given up his life with his ship.

Several crew members from the *Californian*, including that ship's captain, Stanley Lord, gave testimony early in the investigation. Since most people believed that the *Californian* had been near enough to see the rockets, the fact that the ship's log made no reference to them was suspicious. One of the worst crimes known to sailors is a failure to respond to a signal for help. Although it was never conclusively proved, most observers felt that the *Californian*'s log had been altered.

The testimony of the *Californian*'s crew members showed that their ship was "probably" no more than 5 to 10 miles (8 to 16 km) away from the *Titanic* as it lay helpless. Certainly the *Californian* was no farther than 19 miles (30 km) away and could have been on the scene before the *Titanic* sank.

Captain Rostron and his crew on the *Carpathia* came in for high praise, because he and his ship had done as much as was humanly possible to rescue the *Titanic*'s passengers.

Lord Mersey, head of the British Board of Trade's investigation, agreed with many of the findings of the American investigation, including those relating to crew behavior, the lowering of the lifeboats, and the fact that the ship was keeping a very fast speed in dangerous waters.

Both investigators concluded, with only minor differences in details, that the ship had been going too fast in hazardous conditions. And once the iceberg had been struck, the crew had not maintained enough order as passengers began abandoning the ship.

WHAT WAS LEARNED

The British and American investigations both identified certain changes that were needed to make the North Atlantic a safer place for all shipping. After the *Titanic*, the pay for wireless operators was increased substantially and working conditions were improved. From that time on, wireless rooms had to be staffed around the clock. The wireless operator on board the *Californian* had gone to bed shortly after the *Titanic* hit the iceberg. He never knew of the disaster until he turned his radio equipment on again in the morning. By then it was too late.

A much stricter ruling was made about the number of lifeboats available. And from that time forward steamship companies made certain there were enough lifeboats for everyone on board all ships. Within days, several ships hastily added lifeboats to comply with these new rules. Rules for conducting serious lifeboat drills came into force. All nations joined together to make these changes. Never again would international shipping organizations allow ships to sail with inexperienced crews.

New and more demanding shipbuilding specifications were called for. Hull construction was altered so that ships' keels, or bottoms, would be stronger.

As a result of the accident, an organization called the International Ice Patrol was born. Except for the years of the two world wars, this group has been responsible ever since for altering all shipping and for creating maps of potentially dangerous areas in the North Atlantic.

Finally, little attempt was made to rid the public of the notion that steerage passengers had been discriminated against. There was never any proof that third-class passengers had been held back forcibly on the night the *Titanic* went down. It seems they were simply ignored. And much the same indifference was exhibited during both the American and British investigations. If someone had traveled in first class, people paid attention. If they had been in steerage, no one cared.

6

THE YEARS OF SILENCE

It is hard for us to understand the impact the disaster had on the public. The initial press coverage was enormous, and much of it was critical of the wealthy and of the ship that the wealthy had built for their use. Churchmen on both sides of the Atlantic took the rich to task and felt that those who had suffered were only getting what they deserved. A great deal of hellfire and damnation was preached against the rich and powerful.

Many survivors sold their colorful recollections of the *Titanic*'s sinking to newspapers and magazines. Often these stories were short on accuracy and long on embellishment. Tales of dastardly deeds by crew members and wealthy passengers alike circulated. Many people felt that the inspirational stories, truthful or not, were far more satisfying than the ugly tales. Thus a certain glamour, or romance, began to grow up around the hours of the sinking. For a few years following the disaster, references to the *Titanic* continued to make news and hold people's interest, but the headline-grabbing days were over.

Hollywood's version of the ship sinking, Titanic, *released in 1953*

A few days after the *Titanic's* sinking, a small cable ship, the *Mackay-Bennett*, was sent out from Halifax, Nova Scotia. Its sad task was to recover as many bodies as possible from the area where the liner sank. The ship spent two weeks searching and eventually found just over 300 bodies. The ship brought 190 of those bodies back to shore for burial. One of them was John Jacob

Astor. His body was easy to identify because of the initials JJA on his linen shirt. A man reportedly worth $87 million, Astor also carried $2,500 in cash in his pockets. The rest of the bodies were buried at sea.

Survivors and families of those who had perished sued the White Star Line for vast sums of money. But most of the claims were settled privately and for reduced amounts. These suits dragged on until 1916, when they were finally cleared up. For the record, the White Star Line paid a total of only $665,000 in damages. This is a strikingly low figure in light of the original claims totaling some $16 million to $18 million.

Insurance claims covered the loss of most of the ship's cargo, which wasn't particularly rich or remarkable anyway. A value of $420,000 was placed on the contents of the ship's hold. The cargo seemed to be made up of some very ordinary things: sponges, wine, and oak beams, among other items. Other freight included cases of orchids, crates of shelled walnuts, and 900 rolls of linoleum!

One of the single most valuable items was a rare edition of *The Rubaiyat of Omar Khayyam*. This particular copy had a binding encrusted with over a thousand jewels. Stories were told of one passenger who had an $11,000 diamond necklace. A Philadelphia banker had placed gold coins and bullion worth $50,000 in the ship's safe.

One of the rumors that has surrounded the *Titanic*'s sinking was that Captain Smith committed suicide shortly before the ship sank. There were also repeated, but totally unconfirmed, stories that he had survived and spent the rest of his life wandering around the Great Lakes region. No one seemed to ask why Captain Smith, an Englishman, would choose the United States for his final days.

For almost forty years very little was heard about the *Titanic*. From 1915 to 1955 no books were published about the collision. Then in 1955 Walter Lord wrote his account of the sinking, *A Night to Remember*, which re-creates the exciting tale of the *Titanic*'s first and last voyage. For a whole new generation of readers the story took on new importance.

LARGER AND FASTER SHIPS

In the years following the sinking the name *Titanic* came to stand for any kind of major disaster, and the expression "just the tip of the iceberg" suggested that something had hidden dangers. In fact, the larger and most dangerous portions of most icebergs lie well beneath the water's surface.

But horrible as the accident had been, it did not stop anyone from building bigger, faster, and grander ships. Around the corner were the *Berengaria*, the *Leviathan*, and the *Majestic*. The late twenties ushered in the dazzling streamlined German ships, the *Europa* and the *Bremen*. Superliners reached their peak in the middle thirties. Both the *Normandie* and the *Queen Mary* arrived on the scene in the years just before World War II. Even then liners were still the only way to go!

The White Star Line tried to forget the *Titanic*, but it couldn't. The company had planned a third liner to run on the express route between Southampton and New York along with the *Titanic* and the *Olympic*. This ship, the *Britannic*, was launched in 1914, but because of World War I she never saw commercial service. The *Britannic* served as a hospital ship during the war and was destroyed, probably by a mine, in 1916 off the coast of Greece.

Almost immediately after the *Titanic* sank, the *Olympic* had her bulkheads strengthened and the number of lifeboats was increased. She sailed quietly and safely, a popular ship, until she was retired in the early 1930s, a victim of old age and the Depression. But the White Star Line was never quite the same and eventually merged with its rival, Cunard. The Cunard White Star Line was formed, and lasted for a while, but by the end of the 1940s the "White Star" part of the name was absorbed. Cunard Line became the company name, and White Star was gone forever.

Walter Lord's book generated new interest in the ship. Over a hundred books were published and a dozen movies were released in which the *Titanic* was featured. In 1960 a scene in the Broadway musical *The Unsinkable Molly Brown* showed the legendary and eccentric Molly Brown in charge of one of the ship's lifeboats.

In 1963 interested fans joined together to form an organization. By 1974 the group had become strong and large enough to call themselves the Titanic Historical Society, Inc.

As the years went on, more and more of the survivors grew old and many of them died. Each year means fewer and fewer survivors. By 1998 there were just five people alive who had been aboard the ship. Even someone who was on the *Titanic* as a small child would now be close to ninety.

RENEWED INTEREST

As the sixties turned into the seventies, people began to realize that science and technology had made enormous strides. Adventurers began to dream of raising the *Titanic* even though it was probably under 2.5 miles (4 km) of water in the North Atlantic, somewhere off the Grand Banks of Newfoundland.

Some people dreamed of remarkable schemes to raise the ship. Some of the ideas had possibilities and some were preposterous. And even if the ideas were good ones, the cost would be incredible. Very few people

A similar scene, which shows the Titanic's lifeboats being filled, from the British film, A Night to Remember, *released in 1958.*

or organizations could find the money to raise the ship. And before the *Titanic* could be raised, the ship had to be found.

One of the people who was fascinated by the story of the *Titanic* was an Englishman named Douglas Woolley. In the 1960s he devised several schemes for raising the ship. Later, he claimed to have acquired the rights and ownership of the wreck. He managed to get the attention of the news media, but he had a much harder time finding the enormous sums of money it was going to take to make any of his ideas become a reality. And so nothing came of his schemes. But people listened to what he was saying, and they became more and more interested in the possibilities of going down and raising the ship.

A Welshman, John Pierce, planned to raise the hull by attaching canvas bags to it. Hydrogen would then be pumped into the bags and the ship would rise. As recently as 1979 Pierce wanted to wrap the liner in a net. After that he would pump nitrogen into the net. Then the nitrogen would freeze and, like ice cubes in a drink, the ship would float to the surface.

Another person planned to inject ping-pong balls into the ship's hull through a long pipe or hose. Then the ship would float and rise to the top. But no one seemed able to find enough money to fund such an operation.

And then in the early 1980s several people came very close to finding the sunken ship. A wealthy Texas businessman named Jack Grimm spent $2 million on three separate missions that failed to locate the *Titanic*. An ardent adventurer, Grimm had already made attempts to find the Loch Ness Monster and Big Foot.

By donating money for equipment, Grimm got the support of two important research organizations:

Lamont-Doherty Geological Observatory and Scripps Institution of Oceanography. At one point in 1981 Grimm and his team on board the research vessel *Gyre* thought they had sighted one of the ship's three propellers. Grimm and his team were sure the *Titanic* had gone to the bottom of the ocean in one piece. Grimm's team from Columbia University spent part of the summer of 1983 searching, but they ran out of money.

Many people had given up hope that the *Titanic* would ever be located.

THE GREAT SHIP IS FOUND

But then something exciting happened. Suddenly, after eighty-five years, the *Titanic* made newspaper headlines all over again.

A group of scientists who were testing underwater video equipment on board the oceanographic research vessel *Knorr* were just about to finish their day's work. They had spent several weeks in search of the *Titanic* and were getting bored with the routine of their task. Suddenly an object that struck them as familiar flashed across their TV monitors.

Someone ventured out loud that it looked like one of the *Titanic*'s huge boilers. It was an image they had studied from old photographs provided by the ship's builders. It was shortly after 1:00 A.M. on September 1,

1985. Everything began to fall into place. The *Titanic*, or at least some portion of it, had been found.

The *Titanic* was pretty much where everyone thought she would be, 500 miles (800 km) south of Newfoundland. The precise resting place of the ship had always been a little uncertain. The original coordinates had been given as 41 degrees 46 minutes North and 50 degrees 14 minutes West. But no one could ever be sure. Even the slightest deviation from these bearings could mean a variation of many square miles. And there was always the chance that the ship had drifted from this assumed position on its way 2.5 miles (4 km) down to the bottom.

It was the computerized instrument *Argo* that had actually sighted the ship. The size of a small car, the *Argo* weighs 4,000 pounds (1,800 kg). It is attached to the "mother" ship by a thick cable. The vehicle is towed through the ocean, like a sled, from 50 to 100 feet (15 to 30 m) above the ocean bottom. The *Argo* is armed with powerful cameras and strobe lights to light the ocean, which is pitch dark at that depth. There it can take video pictures of objects hidden from normal view and relay them to the surface.

What the *Argo* found was the *Titanic*'s final resting place. The ship was discovered sitting upright but it

One of the first photographs released in 1985 clearly shows the great ship's bow, with the railings virtually intact.

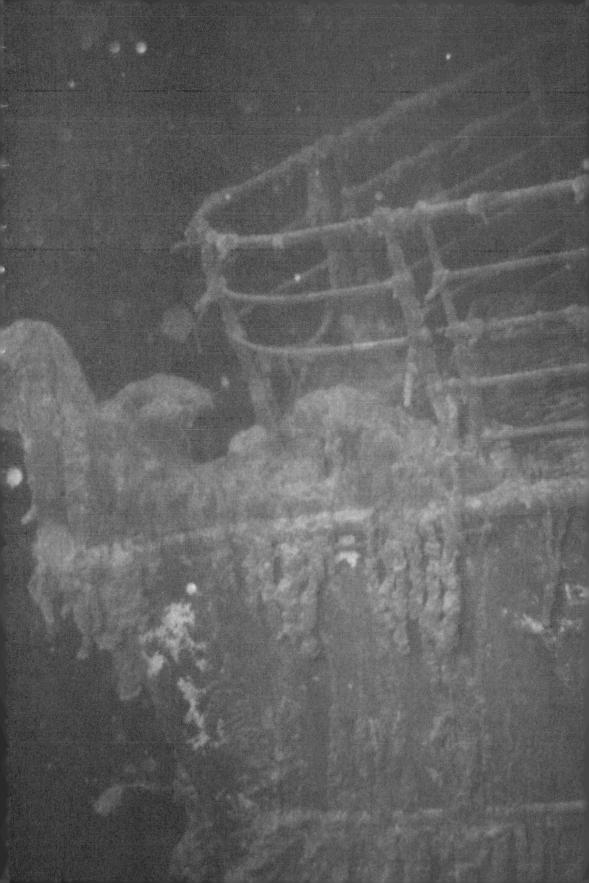

appeared to be in sections. The stern, or rear, section of the ship was about 2,600 feet (800 m) away from the rest of the ship. It seems that the middle portion— covering a length of about 300 feet (90 m)—is still unaccounted for. It may have broken up on the way down and then disintegrated. This "middle" break probably occurred because of the many open spaces in the center of the ship.

All four of the majestic funnels were missing. At one point the *Argo* bumped into part of the ship's superstructure. When the instrument resurfaced there was a smudge of black paint on its surface.

Once the ship was found, another vehicle was pressed into service. Over a period of five days, ANGUS, an even smaller instrument, made three trips to the site. Also towed along like a sled attached to the support ship, ANGUS took color photographs. During these trips, both ANGUS and the *Argo* took more than twelve thousand photographs, many of which would appear in newspapers and magazines as news of the ship's discovery became known.

The discovery of the *Titanic* was due in large part to the persistence of Robert D. Ballard, a marine geologist from the Woods Hole Oceanographic Institution, and head of the institution's Deep Submergence Laboratory. An untiring worker, Ballard became interested in the *Titanic* through a friend. Using his skills as a scientist and engineer he helped to develop the *Argo*, primarily for searching for underwater objects.

Ballard and his team of scientists, and a group of French oceanographers from the Research Institute for the Exploration of the Sea (IFREMER), had spent several weeks narrowing the position of the *Titanic* down from 150 square miles (390 sq km) to 30 square miles (80 sq km). At that point the *Argo* could be used to locate the wreck visually.

In 1985 there was intense excitement over the discovery and the photographing of the lost wreck after all the years of mystery. There was enthusiasm that the ship seemed to be so well preserved, even though it was in pieces. In the "debris field" between the front and rear portions of the ship, photographs were taken of bedsprings, silver serving trays and ice buckets, chamber pots, and suitcases. All the objects were lying on the ocean floor, and many of them seemed to be in excellent condition.

NEW QUESTIONS ASKED

Within a month of the discovery Ballard appeared before Congress to request that the *Titanic* be made an International Memorial. This designation would keep the wreck safe from treasure hunters and looters, even though the expense of getting down to the ship would be prohibitive for most people.

But was there any treasure to be found? Some people estimated that the gold and silver left on the ship would fetch hundreds of millions of dollars. But that is mostly speculation. No one really knows for sure. The cargo manifest itself shows few riches. And while some of the ship is in first-rate condition, other parts of it seem completely ruined.

Nobody is quite sure who owns what is left of the *Titanic*. In 1985 a British court ruled that Great Britain had no claims to a wreck in international waters. And all the insurance claims have long since been settled. A British company, Commercial Union, may have some legal claim to the ship's contents. They were not the original insurers but are the successors to the company that handled the original claims. Cunard Line, which eventually came to own the White Star Line, does not feel that it owns the ship.

The discovery of the *Titanic* started people thinking once more about the future of the vessel. Some people feel that the ship ought to be left as it was found, as a memorial to the people who lost their lives in 1912. And others want to bring some of the artifacts to the surface for history's sake. In many ways it appears that there is a very thin line that distinguishes underwater treasure hunters from those who believe in preserving the past for its own sake.

Shortly after the September 1 discovery of the *Titanic* a group of people stood on the stern of the *Knorr*. They were on the surface just about over the spot where the great ship had gone down. It was late at night, almost at the same hour that seventy-three years earlier the *Titanic* had begun to lose its struggle against the ominously still Atlantic waters. The group held a memorial service for those lost in the disaster.

8 THE STORY CONTINUES

Almost as soon as the 1985 dives were over, Ballard and his team began to make plans for a return visit in 1986. Although he wanted to leave the vessel as it had been found, Ballard was determined to be on board a manned submersible that would descend the next summer and get close to the wreck.

And that is exactly what happened. During eleven days in July 1986, Ballard and his team went down to photograph the *Titanic* even more closely than they had the summer before.

This time they were aided by the *Alvin*, a twenty-year-old submersible capable of holding three people. Initially designed to descend to about 6,000 feet (1,800 m), the vessel had been completely reinforced so that she could go down comfortably to 13,000 feet (3,900 m).

It took the fifty-six researchers four days to sail the research vessel *Atlantis II* from Woods Hole Oceanographic Institution in Massachusetts to the *Titanic* site.

Each day followed a similar pattern: the *Alvin* would begin its two-and-a-half-hour descent to the *Titanic* shortly after breakfast. The submersible spent about four hours of the day at the bottom, followed by the two-and-a-half-hour ascent back to the *Atlantis II*. Attached to the *Alvin* by a tether was a new remotely operated instrument: Jason Junior, known as JJ.

On the third day this camera-equipped robot actually entered the liner's interior. There, in the great liner's grand ballroom, JJ took the now famous photographs of one of the ship's crystal light fixtures. JJ was the first "visitor" to the ship since April of 1912.

A deep-diving robot developed for the U.S. Navy, JJ is about the size of a lawn mower. It weighs about 250 pounds (113 kg) and was attached to the *Alvin* by a 250-foot-long (75 m) electric cable. The 20-inch-high (50 cm) by 24-inch-wide (60 cm) apparatus is small enough to fit into places where none of the previous instruments could go. It takes high-resolution color photos and video pictures. On the 1986 mission the video images were then transmitted back to the three crew members inside the *Alvin*.

JJ's photographs helped to clear up more elements of the mystery. The grand staircase was there, minus the wood. All non-metal objects seemed to have disappeared, eaten away by marine organisms over the years. But most of the metal remains well preserved.

Ballard discovered, however, that much of the iron hull
plating is covered with what he describes as "rustsicles."

JJ's pictures also made clear where the ship had split
apart: just in front of the third funnel. Even more objects
were found in 1986 on the ocean floor in the space
between the two parts of the ship: a doll's head, shoes,
and four of the ship's safes. The *Alvin*'s robot arm tried
to open one of the safes, but nothing would budge the
rusted door. By and large the objects strewn on the

The research vessel Atlantis II *and its manned submersible* Alvin

ocean floor were those belonging to steerage passengers, not first- or second-class ones.

NEW EVIDENCE

Eleven days, sixty hours, and more than sixty thousand still photos later, JJ had completed its task. Some other things became clearer in the 1986 photos. It was determined that the stern section had swiveled 180

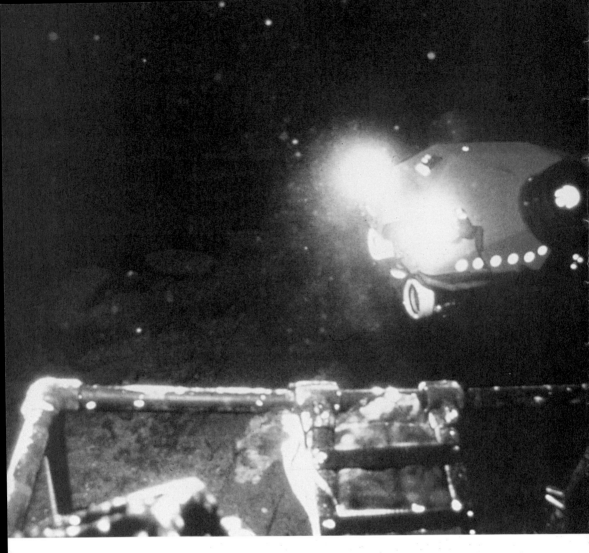

The robot JJ leaves the manned submersible Alvin *and sets out for a day's work photographing the remains of the* Titanic.

degrees after breaking away at or near the surface. The remains of the stern section are heavily damaged and have many sharp parts that make exploration, even by a robot, hazardous. There was always the worry that the tether line would get caught.

The most significant finding of all was that there is no sign of the 300-foot-long (90 m) gash that had always been accepted as the reason the *Titanic* sank. What Ballard found instead was evidence of buckled and torn plates of the metal sheathing on the ship's hull. This damage must have occurred when the *Titanic* struck the iceberg.

The bow is now buried in 50 feet (15 m) of silt and mud, almost up to the anchors. Just at the point where the ship broke apart, Ballard was able to see the buckled plates and sheared rivets below the waterline. These "tears" were near the fins that had been designed to minimize rolling of the vessel. They would have been enough to send the ship to the bottom. It is also possible, however, that some of these plates were torn when the ship actually hit the ocean bottom.

Most people are now convinced that the *Titanic*'s split and broken hull could not and should not be salvaged. Ballard feels it would be impossible since the bow is broken in several places. But Jack Grimm was determined to dive for artifacts to bring back. He was the first to admit, however, that exceptionally expensive diving would be required.

Running the *Alvin* is an expensive proposition. It costs about $20,000 a day to operate the submersible and "mother" ship. The total cost of operating JJ for the twelve days was $220,000; this was funded by the U.S. Navy. The *Alvin*'s crew can stay down only a few hours before the limited battery supply of oxygen is used up. The *Alvin* is also very slow, going only at about 1 mile

(1.6 km) an hour. Any other available submersibles would be just as costly.

As a result of the 1985 and 1986 dives, Ballard and his researchers were able to piece together a "mosaic" picture, joining photographs of small sections of the *Titanic* to make a recognizable whole. In this way the liner can be studied more carefully and perhaps even more can be learned about exactly why and how she went down.

On the *Alvin's* seventh dive, Ballard and his team placed a memorial plaque donated by the *Titanic* Historical Society on the sunken vessel. It was left on the ship's stern, the last part of the ship to remain afloat. It was also the place where the largest number of people died. The inscription on it read, in part:

In memory of those souls who perished with the Titanic, April 14-15, 1912.

The sentiment speaks for many people who believe that we have learned all that the *Titanic* can teach us. Ballard felt that he and his team had found as much information was needed. As far as he was concerned, his work was done.

TEN YEARS LATER

9

True to his word, Ballard has yet to go back to the ocean floor where the *Titanic* still lies. Instead he has lectured and written about the ship and his work on the discovery of the vessel. And he has been vocal about leaving the wreck of the ship and its contents on the ocean floor, just as it is.

But others have not been as principled. Indeed, the French-based part of the original Woods Hole team, IFREMER, broke off from Ballard's group. They soon joined forces with an organization known as R.M.S. *Titanic* Inc. to return to the *Titanic*'s grave. In 1987 the group went down and retrieved some 2,000 objects from the ocean floor and from the ship itself. These were brought up, cleaned, and put on display in various sites. And in the fall of that year, a television show hosted by the late actor Telly Savalas showed many of these objects. On the same show there was a live segment where a briefcase, long at the bottom of the ocean, was to be opened for the first time since 1912. When opened, the briefcase turned out to have absolutely nothing inside!

Titanica, a 70-millimeter giant-screen documentary, was the result of seventeen dives to the Titanic in 1991. A joint Russian-Canadian venture, two submersibles dived down to the wreck for a total of 140 hours. When the film is shown on a giant IMAX screen, the documentary presents stunning close-up views of the wreck on the ocean bottom.

TO DIVE OR NOT TO DIVE?

For the first time, many people began to fully understand Ballard's request to leave the *Titanic* and its contents alone, to rest in quiet dignity. In fact, a motion was put in front of the U.S. Congress proposing a law that stated that the "sale or display for profit" of any *Titanic* memorabilia in the United States was illegal. Even R.M.S. Titanic Inc. has pledged to leave the ship alone and to retrieve only those artifacts lying in the debris surrounding the pieces of the ship. The organization has also said that it will only display such objects and not sell them.

The group returned to the bottom of the North Atlantic two more times, in 1993 and 1994. By the time they were finished, divers had brought up almost 4,000 items, including shoes, wine and beer bottles, fine china, and crystal. With French help, many of these objects were painstakingly restored. In the fall of 1994, a major *Titanic* exhibit—including a small sampling of these objects—opened at the National Maritime Museum in Greenwich, England. During the course of the show's year-long run, more than 700,000 visitors paid to see the exhibit.

Once more controversy arose. Was it right to make a commercial venture out of historic artifacts from such a devastating tragedy? Even the few remaining survivors

The metal steering mechanism on the ship's bridge. The bridge itself and all the surroundings were made of wood and have been completely eaten away by marine organisms.

had differing opinions about the morality of such an exhibit. Some were in favor of it, but others, such as Eva Hart, said shortly before she died in 1996, "The ship is its own memorial. Leave it there."

But worthwhile scientific information also came out of some of these commercial events. Researchers cast doubt in 1993 on the quality of the steel used in the building of the *Titanic*. From samples brought up in 1987, IFREMER was able to state that the steel used in the ship may not have been of the highest grade. The steel had a high sulfur content, which sometimes causes the metal to break apart. And when combined with the near freezing sea and air temperatures that fateful night, the steel became "brittle," in the words of research scientists. Had the steel been stronger, it was stated, the damage to the ship's hull might not have been so severe. So now there was something else to add to the litany of things that had gone wrong on the night of April 14, 1912.

In the summer of 1996 the organization called R.M.S. *Titanic* Inc. sponsored a dive to bring up a section of the ship's hull. The plan was to hoist up an eleven-ton segment and use it as part of a permanent *Titanic* exhibit. As part of this questionable task, two large cruise liners sailed from Boston and New York. The ships carried some 1,500 passengers, who had paid up to $10,000 to witness the event, and they were eager to be on site when the section of the hull was raised.

A White Star Line mug (above) and several pieces of rusted silverware (below) were among the items found during many dives to the wreck of the ship.

Underwater cameras were on hand to record the salvage operation.

But heavy seas and strong winds intervened, and as the section of the hull came within about 200 feet (60 m) of the ocean's surface, the cable snapped and the piece, which measured 24 by 20 feet (7-1/2 x 6 m), went plummeting back down to the bottom. Disappointment prevailed, not only among the organizers and financiers, but also among the cruise passengers. On one of the ships was 99-year-old *Titanic* survivor, Edith Brown Haisman. Although old and frail, Mrs. Haisman still was able to relive memories of that cold April evening when the great ship went down.

THE LATEST FINDINGS

As a result of the many dives to the *Titanic*, scientists were able in 1997 and 1998 to make further new discoveries about the ship's sinking. For most of the eighty-five years that had passed since the ship went down, the theory was that the iceberg had ripped a 300-foot-(90-m)-long gash in the ship's hull. Now scientists and engineers were able to back up Ballard's claim that this was not so. They seemed to feel that the iceberg had

Survivor Edith Haisman visits the
Titanic *exhibit in Greenwich, England.*

made only six fairly small slits in the side of the ship's hull. The combined size of these holes is estimated to be 12 to 13 square feet (1.1 to 1.2 sq m). But because these holes occurred just above the height of the watertight compartments, the ship was doomed.

Because the ship's forward section is buried deep in mud at the ocean's bottom, the scientists were totally dependent on sonar readings to make this discovery. Because the holes were so small, the water rushed into the ship's bottom at very high pressure—something like the way water comes out of a fire hose. In fact, this idea was put forth at the British Inquiry in 1912, but no one then would believe that such small holes could sink the ship.

Scientists estimate that up to 40,000 tons of water poured into the Titanic's hull before she sank in just under two hours. The results of these and other findings were shown on the Discovery Channel in a documentary called "Titanic: Anatomy of a Disaster."

To this day, one thing that almost all scientists agree about is that if the ship had been going slower, the damage would not have been so severe, and the great ship might have stayed afloat and been saved from plunging to the ocean floor.

There is little reason to expect that the wreck of the Titanic will remain well preserved forever. Although most organic substances—such as wood and cloth—have already been eaten away by sea creatures, there's a good chance that even the steel, surrounded by so much water, will begin to disintegrate. Already rust has formed in many places. One scientist says that even now as much as 20 percent of the ship's hull has been eaten away by microbes.

In 1998 another new discovery was made. It is now believed that many of the rivets that were used to keep the steel plates of the ship fastened together "popped" when the *Titanic* hit the iceberg. And several of these rivets, brought up from the ocean bottom, have been tested. Studies show a high concentration of slag, a glassy waste material that is a by-product of steel production. Combined with the poor quality steel, the quality of the rivets shows that in many ways the structural materials used in building the *Titanic* were probably inferior.

Although only two rivets have so far been examined by the National Institute of Standards and Technology, the preliminary evidence is stunning. The presence of slag is three times greater than in modern steel-making procedures. It is still not clear, however, if the rivets in the *Titanic* were typical of all steel made at that time and were therefore not necessarily inferior.

All these new discoveries indicate that there is still much being learned—and many long-standing myths are being shattered—due to modern technology and also due to the high-tech expeditions. Everything seems to send mixed messages: Divers go to retrieve artifacts, (which many people think is wrong), yet some of their discoveries yield critical new scientific data about what went wrong and caused the ship to sink so quickly (and most people feel that gathering such knowledge is all right).

10

STAR OF STAGE AND SCREEN

Since the discovery of the ship's location in 1985, the public's fascination with the *Titanic* and what happened to it on the night of April 14 has rarely faltered. In fact, in recent years interest in the topic seems to have grown and grown. Many documentaries and several fictionalized mini series and TV shows have been produced and shown to varying degrees of success.

ON STAGE

In 1997 a major Broadway musical named *Titanic* was announced. How could such an action-packed story be realized within the confines of a theater? How could music, singing, and dancing be appropriate to tell one of the most tragic stories of the twentieth century, if not of all time? And how did anyone have the audacity to show a sinking ship on a small stage?

Indeed, Broadway gossips began to circulate rumors almost as soon as the production was announced to open at New York City's Lunt-Fontanne Theater on April 23, 1997. It was too tempting to imagine Broadway headlines: "New *Titanic* Musical Sinks Upon Opening." And indeed, the first several previews of the show were cancelled "for technical reasons." In theater lore, this usually means a show is in deep trouble. Rumors grew and grew. What was really wrong with the production? And would the new show even open?

But the rumors were, happily, unfounded. With a very complicated set and lighting setup, the show did indeed have just that: technical difficulties. And when the musical was actually ready to be seen by paying audiences, word spread that the show actually had something going for it. During the preview period, changes were made, songs were added, and the script was rewritten and the direction was tightened. Such changes are typical of most shows—even ones that go on to become the biggest hits.

By opening night, audiences had grown very enthusiastic about the whole show. And critics, pretty much, were equally surprised by the musical. Everyone

Cast members board the ship in the musical Titanic.

seemed astonished that the show was not the disaster that had been expected. All the elements worked together, and the tragic moments were handled with dignity and taste. In Act 2, after the ship hits the iceberg, the sets tilted, suggesting the sinking ship. A drink trolley sails from one side of the stage to the other, a highly effective way of letting everyone in the audience know that the ship is tilting and in peril.

In June of 1997, many people were pleasantly surprised when the show won five Tony Awards, including the most important one: the Best Musical of 1997. These awards, equivalent to Hollywood's Oscars, were named for an active theater figure, Antoinette ("Tony") Perry. A live scene was shown on the TV award ceremonies, and this, coupled with the Best Musical Award, helped the show become the major sellout attraction it hadn't been up to that point.

ON SCREEN

But the best was yet come. Due to be released as one of the big summer movies of 1997, James Cameron's long-awaited film, *Titanic*, was suddenly delayed until Christmas. Again, the Hollywood pundits had a field day. Movie prophets smelled a major disaster. Was this going to be an even bigger cataclysm than the original sinking of the *Titanic*? Rumors circulated around Hollywood talking of a major flop in the film industry. Would the movie become the most expensive disaster of all time?

Production costs had soared, and at $200 million, the *Titanic* was the most expensive movie ever made. Indeed, so large was its budget—and so often had the budget grown—that two studios were required to handle all the expenses of production and distribution. Both Paramount and 20th Century Fox were announced as co-producers.

But on December 19, 1997 the film opened, to largely excellent reviews, and the public flocked to it. It remained the Number 1 box office attraction up until Oscar night, and by the same date it had become, in what is a very short time, the Number 1 all-time domestic grossing film, outgrossing even such popular movies as *Star Wars, ET,* and *Jurassic Park.*

A hit all over the world, the movie had grossed $1.2 billion worldwide by Oscar night, a modern-day box office record. Over and above that income there is still the home video market. As well, NBC has reportedly paid $30 million to show the movie on TV in 2000.

Despite a running length of 3 hours and 17 minutes, the film became a huge popular success. Many young people saw the movie two and three (and even more) times, and lead actor Leonardo DiCaprio became the teenage girl's heartthrob. Not far behind in popularity was the young English actress, Kate Winslet, cast opposite DiCaprio as the American heiress, Rose,

who falls in love with the impoverished artist.

Meanwhile, the soundtrack album, featuring the hit song, "My Heart Will Go On," sung by Celine Dion, became the first movie album to hit #1 on the charts since *Chariots of Fire* in 1981. And, as long as the film itself remained #1 at the box office, the album and song stood alongside in popularity.

Director and writer Cameron had gone to great trouble to make an authentic film. From pre-production to shooting, the movie took almost four years to make. In an effort to study his subject with utmost care and respect, Cameron made twelve dives down to the *Titanic*. Each trip lasted from ten to twelve hours, not counting the time it took him to get down and return. He and his team used the two Russian submersibles that had filmed the IMAX movie in 1991.

On the ocean floor, Cameron's team photographed many hours of *Titanic* images. Although Ballard had declared that there was no wood left on the ship, Cameron and his crew found the remains of several oak columns in the ship's reception room. They had been painted, and Cameron's theory was that the paint contained so much lead that marine organisms ignored the wood.

The Russian submersible Mir II about to dive to the Titanic. This vehicle, used to make the IMAX film Titanica, was one of the submersibles used by Cameron when he was researching the wreck for his movie.

Once Cameron had made his preliminary dives and had done his underwater research on the wreck, he prepared to build a life-size replica of the *Titanic*. This was done in Baja California in Mexico, a part of the world that doesn't much resemble the chilly North Atlantic. The ship model sat in a specially built drydock. The result was a painstakingly real reproduction of the ship.

To save money, the outside of the model was completed only on one side—the starboard (right) side. Any images that needed to be shot on the ship's port (left) side had to be reversed, or "flopped." This means the camera's image was turned around to fill out the missing half. Computers spliced the images together. One such shot is early in the movie, sailing day from Southampton, when all the passengers see the *Titanic* for the first time. The set for this scene also turned out to be the largest in motion picture history.

All the ship's interiors were reproduced with equal attention to detail and accuracy. Interior room decorations were studied carefully from old photographs, and as a result, suites, staterooms, corridors, and public rooms all bear a strong degree of authenticity. Much the same attitude prevailed when it came to simulating the china, silverware, baggage, and costumes of the 1912 Edwardian period. The *Titanic*'s builders, Harland and Wolff, lent as much archival material as they possessed, including blueprints and designs long thought lost.

Smaller scale models of the ship were also built, and through state-of-the-art digital computer technology, shots of the different models were combined to provide thrilling images of the great ship in different situations. Computer technology also came into play when shooting the ship's collision with the iceberg. It was also used for the climactic scenes as the ship starts to sink. It allowed passengers to be filmed separately and then, superimposed, shown sliding down the rear section of the ship. This was nothing new, but Cameron used computer-generated images on such a large scale and with such sophistication that the resulting special effects are a new dimension in modern moviemaking.

In addition to the speaking actors in the movie, there was a core group of 150 extras, who stayed with the movie the entire time it was being filmed. As part of his bid for absolute accuracy, Cameron had made sure that these people all understood how to walk properly, wear clothes, and move and behave like real people in 1912 society.

Cameron then broke up the full-size model into sections to show in the closing scenes of the ship sinking. In these scenes, many additional extras and stunt people were used in order to create an accurate sense of pandemonium—and doom. Most of the film was shot on sets with reproductions of 1912 life, and most of the water scenes originated in four different sized tanks, one of which held 17 million gallons of water.

Cameron's intention was to create a fictional love story set against the human tragedy of the factual sinking. And judging from the movie's phenomenal success, audiences have responded to just that blend. When all is said and done, it is the continuing allure of the *Titanic*'s story that has made the tale of its tragic ending so popular for over eighty-five years. It is the lore of the ship itself that has kept the *Titanic* in the public eye for all that time.

EPILOGUE

In the years following the sinking of the great liner, the name *Titanic* has become synonymous with catastrophic disaster. But is that really an accurate depiction of the ship's legacy?

Consider Walter Lord, whose brilliant chronicle of the events on April 14, 1912, *A Night to Remember*, continues to sell steadily more than four decades after it was originally published. Consider the stage production of *Titanic*, which was supposed to flop—and was instead christened the Best Musical of 1997. And most important, consider the success of writer-director James Cameron, whose own *Titanic* project has allowed him to join the ranks of Steven Spielberg and George Lucas as one of the most profitable filmmakers of the twentieth century. Even at the time of the sinking, any newspaper that included the word *Titanic* in its headlines was sure to sell. And in the modern era, the ship continues to be a source of interest on the Internet, where even a quick search will reveal several dozen *Titanic* sites.

It would appear, ironically, that the *Titanic* is in fact one of the most successful "disasters" of all time. Why? Because the story of the *Titanic* is one loaded with optimism, suspense, and heartbreak—all the elements of great drama. Like all good stories, it will continue to be told to generation after generation of fascinated audiences.

Eighty-five years ago there were hundreds of ships of all kinds and sizes sailing between England and the United States. Today there is only one luxury liner crossing the Atlantic from New York on a regular basis. Only the *Queen Elizabeth II* sails on that route, and then only occasionally. The only people who can go to Europe by boat these days are either terrified of flying or can afford to spend a week in the hotel-like luxury of the *Queen Elizabeth II*. The superliner is almost as extinct as the dinosaur.

Audiences at the *Titanic* musical can see, in the lobby of the Lunt-Fontanne Theater, hundreds of names written on the wall. A closer look reveals that the names are in fact a list of the passengers aboard the *Titanic* for its doomed maiden voyage. Some of the names are marked by an asterisk to indicate survivors of the disaster. It is a touching reminder for the people about to enjoy a glitzy, multimillion-dollar Broadway show that the characters they see on stage were once very real and very much alive.

TITANIC TRIVIA

Finding no chance to advance his naval career, Charles H. Lightoller retired to England in the 1920s. But he reappeared during World War II, when he rescued more than 130 British soldiers from the Germans during the Battle of Dunkirk.

The British and American inquiries produced more than 2,000 pages of testimony for future research and interest.

Three million rivets were used to hold the ship together.

In the *Titanic*'s kitchens there were, among other provisions, 75,000 pounds of fresh meat, 1,500 gallons of fresh milk, 40 tons of potatoes, and 600 pounds of butter.

S.O.S. Titanic, a 1979 made-for-TV movie, shot all its exterior scenes on board the R.M.S. *Queen Mary*, retired and moored at Long Beach, California. With its three red-and-black funnels and curved superstructure, the liner is a poor substitute for the *Titanic*'s sharper angles.

More than 6,000 tablecloths and 45,000 table napkins were on board to decorate the ship's dining rooms.

This soap advertisement from 1912 shows that the public found the Titanic fascinating even then.

The pictures that the character played by Leonardo DiCaprio draws in the film *Titanic* were actually drawn by James Cameron, the movie's writer-director.

The rudder at the back that steered the ship weighed just over 100 tons.

There were thirteen honeymoon couples on board the *Titanic*.

There were thirty-one maids, valets, and governesses aboard the ship. This meant that every fourth or fifth family was attended by some kind of servant.

In order to serve meals to passengers in all three classes, there were about 12,000 dinner plates, 2,000 wineglasses, and some 8,000 dinner forks.

Once the *Titanic* sank underwater, it probably took the ship about fifteen minutes to plunge to her final resting place on the ocean bottom. This meant that the ship was descending at roughly 10 miles (16 km) per hour.

Shortly after the *Titanic* rumors began to circulate that a replacement ship would be built. Her name? *Gigantic*.

GLOSSARY

Boat deck. A deck on a ship, usually above the promenade deck, where the lifeboats are usually stowed.

Bow. The front, pointed end of a ship.

Crow's nest. An open receptacle halfway up the forward mast that could usually hold two people, who served as lookouts.

Davit. A vertical metal support, to which a ship's lifeboat is attached at either end.

Edwardian. The period in English history, from 1901 to 1910, which marks the reign of King Edward VII.

Extras. People used in moviemaking, who generally fill out crowd scenes and mostly have no lines to speak.

Flagship. The most important—and usually largest—vessel of a shipping company.

Keel. The bottommost part of a ship, running from bow to stern.

Knot. One nautical mile, or 6,076 feet (1,852 m), per hour. It is slightly longer than a land mile. A knot is the traditional way that a ship's speed, in hours, is measured.

Mast. Most steamships of the early twentieth century carried a mast at the front of the ship and one at the rear. They were holdovers from the days of sailing ships, when several masts were necessary to handle the sails' riggings. By the time of the *Titanic*, masts were still used for some wiring and rigging, but their existence was primarily for the sake of appearance.

Port. If you are standing on a ship and facing the front, the left-hand side of the ship is called the port side.

Promenade deck. One of the main decks of a ship. On the *Titanic*, the deck was glass enclosed for comfortable walking in all kinds of weather. Most of the first-class public rooms were on this deck.

Propeller. Also know as a screw (because of the scientific principle on which it works). The *Titanic* had three propellers that drove the ship. She was therefore referred to as a "triple-screw" ship.

Rudder. A large, flat piece of metal under the stern of a ship that is used for steering.

Sister ship. A second ship that is similar, but not always identical, to another ship. The *Olympic* and *Titanic* were sister ships and looked very alike. But the *Titanic* measured about a thousand tons more, and there were subtle differences between them.

Starboard. If you are standing on a ship and facing the front, the right-hand side of the ship is called the starboard side. Another way to remember: the letter R (for right) is directly next to the letter S (for starboard) in the alphabet.

Steerage. The lowest class of passage on a ship. On many ships, people were thrown into cabins for twelve or more. Because the *Titanic* was a brand new ship, her steerage accommodations were fairly clean and comfortable.

Stern. The back end of a ship is known as the stern.

Submersible. A craft designed to spend varying amounts of time underwater.

Waterline. The bottom of the *Titanic* was painted red, and the sides of the ship were black. The division, where those lines met, was the waterline, and indicated how the ship should "ride" in the water.

FOR FURTHER INFORMATION

Books for Young Readers

There are surprisingly few books about the *Titanic* specifically geared for young readers.
One is Shelley Tanaka's *On Board the Titanic*, A Hyperion/Madison Press Book published in 1996. An account of one of the survivors, Jack Thayer, the book is illustrated with many of Ken Marschall's rightfully famous paintings. Another popular title is Eve Bunting's *SOS Titanic*, an engrossing novel that shows up the class differences on the boat. It was published by Harcourt Brace in 1996.

Adult Books

Because there are so many fine books that deal with different aspects of the *Titanic*, this list is only a selection of what is currently and widely available.

Archbold, Rick. *Last Dinner on the Titanic.* New York: A Hyperion/Madison Press Book, 1997. A delightful reconstruction concerning food—in all three classes—on the *Titanic,* and how it was prepared, made, and served. Modern recipes based on menu items are included. Walter Lord has written the introduction.

Eaton, John P. and Charles A. Haas. *Titanic: Triumph and Tragedy. A Chronicle in Words and Pictures.* Wellingborough, England: Patrick Stephens, 1986. An invaluable book to the *Titanic* buff, this 320-page volume is illustrated with hundreds of archival photographs and accounts of the tragedy.

Lord, Walter. *A Night to Remember* (1955) and *The Night Lives On* (1986). Both of these modern classics are in paperback editions and are readily available, although *A Night to Remember* is still so popular in 1998 that it is frequently out of stock.

Lynch, Don. *Titanic: An Illustrated History.* New York: A Hyperion/Madison Press Book, 1992. Perhaps the definitive book about the ill-fated liner. It is wonderfully detailed and fascinating to read. Ken Marschall's stunning paintings are the visual focus, and Robert D. Ballard has written an eloquent introduction.

Marcus, Geoffrey. *The Maiden Voyage.* New York: The Viking Press, 1969. Another classic, this book is worth searching for.

Marsh, Ed W. *James Cameron's Titanic.* New York: Harper Perennial, 1997. The "souvenir" book of the film, which includes just about everything you would want to know about the movie, the script, the actors, and, not incidentally, the history of the original ship.

Tibballs, Geoff. *The Titanic: The Story of the "Unsinkable" Ship.* Pleasantville, New York: The Reader's Digest Association, Inc., 1997. A good, all-round look at the adventure story surrounding the great liner.

Pamphlets and Brochures

There are an amazing number of pamphlets and brochures published about the sinking of the *Titanic*. Many of them are reprints of first-hand accounts of the sinking by passengers and the few officers who survived. They make fascinating if not always reliable reading. In one of them, *The Sinking of the Titanic and Great Sea Disasters*, the copyright is 1912. The introduction, a "spiritual consolation," is dated April 18, 1912, just three days after the liner sank.

Titanic Historical Society

A small museum and store stock a great deal of *Titanic* memorabilia. Or write to:
Titanic Historical Society
PO Box 51053
Indian Orchard, MA 01151-0053
Web Site: http://www2.titanic1.org/titanic1

Web Sites

Some of the current web sites include:
Official Titanic Movie Site
http://www.titanicmovie.com

Britannica Online
http://www.eb.com

Molly Brown House Museum
http://www.mollybrown.com

Robert Ballard's Jason Project
http://www.jasonproject.org/expedition.html

Discovery Channel Online
http://www.discovery.com/area/science/titanic/titanicopen er.html

CDs

The movie soundtrack album is on Sony Classical.

The single "My Heart Will Go On," sung by Celine Dion, is on the 550 Music label.

The original cast album for the musical, *Titanic*, is on RCA Victor. Its number is 09026-68834-2.

An interesting album is *Music As Heard on the Fateful Voyage*. A group calling itself the White Star Orchestra performs selections as they might have been performed on board the *Titanic*. The orchestra consists of cello, violins, bass, and piano. Wonderfully packaged, the album is a nostalgic treat.

INDEX